The Little Book of

St. Vincent
de Paul

Introduced by
Sr. Catherine Prendergast, D.C.

Compiled by

GW00640786

First published in 2005 by
a little book company
11 Hillsbrook Crescent, Perrystown,
Dublin 12, Ireland.
Email: info@alittlebookcompany.com

 In association with the Daughters of
Charity of St. Vincent de Paul

Compilation copyright © 2005, Don Mullan
ISBN 0-9547047-6-2

Designed & typeset by David Houlden,
PageWorks

Printed by Webcom, Canada

To

*All the Members
and
Associates
of
the Vincentian Family
throughout the World*

Acknowledgements:

The publisher and editor gratefully acknowledge the permission of the Daughters of Charity of St. Vincent de Paul for permission to quote material in their copyright from the following sources: *Spiritual Writings of Louise de Marillac — Correspondence and Thoughts*, Edited and Translated from the French by Sr. Louise Sullivan, D.C., New City Press, Brooklyn, New York, 1991. Copyright: Daughters of Charity, Albany, New York. Translated from the original French edition *Sainte Louise de Marillac: Ecrits Spirituels*. *The Conferences of St. Vincent de Paul to the Daughters of Charity*, Translated from the French by Joseph Leonard, C.M., Collins Liturgical Publications 1979, Copyright translation 1938–1940, The Sisters of Charity of St. Vincent de Paul; *Conferences of Saint Vincent de Paul*, Compiled by Pierre Coste, C.M., Translated by Joseph Leonard, C.M., Edited Eastern Province, U.S.A, 1963; *Saint Vincent de Paul — Correspondence, Conferences, Documents Volume I (1607–1639)*, Translated from the 1920 Edition of Pierre Coste, C.M. by Sr. Helen Marie Law, D.C., Sr. John Marie Poole, D.C., Rev. James R. King, C.M., and Rev. Francis Germovnik, C.M. (Latin), Annotated by: Rev. John W. Carven, C.M.; New City Press, Brooklyn, New York, 1983; *Letters of St. Vincent de Paul*, Translated by Joseph Leonard, C.M., Burns Oates and Washbourne Ltd., London, 1937.

Introduction
ST. VINCENT DE PAUL

St. Vincent de Paul was the living revelation of the New Testament adage 'Faith Without Works is Dead' (James 2: 26). Vincent was a holy and contemplative man who saw the need for an urgent regeneration of the French Church, which he recognised to be in a lamentable state of affairs. He began monthly and weekly retreats as a means of helping to refocus vocations and enable a transfusion of God's grace through prayer and reflection. However, Vincent also saw that love of God required a practical demonstration and that the face of God was to be found amongst the poor and brutalised of French colonial society.

Vincent was born on 24 April 1581 in the village of Pouy, in Gascony. He was the third child of a family of six children. His parents were peasant farmers and he spent many long days and nights tending livestock. Aged 12, through the generosity of a lawyer, he began his education under the Franciscans in Dax. It was here he began to consider the religious life and went on to study at the University of Toulouse. In 1600, he was ordained at the very young age of 19. During his life he counted among his friends St. Francis de Sales.

In 1608, he became chaplain to Queen Marguerite. During this appointment he spent enormous energy distributing alms and tending the sick. He befriended the wretched of French society and was particularly distressed at the suffering of galley slaves, often left to rot in French prisons.

He felt called to demonstrate the practical compassion and mercy of God. He established several Confraternities of Charity which today are known as AIC, *International*

Association of Charity, Amongst his collabora-
tors was Mademoiselle de Gras, the future St.
Louise de Marillac, co-founder with Vincent of
the Daughters of Charity.

Vincent began a religious congregation
known as the Vincentians. Many groups
honour St. Vincent, as their patron including
the Society of St. Vincent de Paul, founded in
Paris in 1833 by Frederic Ozanam. All are
dedicated to alleviation of distress amongst the
poor and abandoned.

Vincent spent many hours each day
engaging in correspondence with the powerful
and the poor. Many of the quotations in this
small volume are taken from his letters. While
written four centuries ago, his comments and
advice are often contemporary: 'People are
ruined by lawsuits.'

It is recalled that when rioting mobs broke
into the Pantheon in Paris during the French

Revolution, they engaged in the destruction of many religious objects. However, the memory of St. Vincent's compassion for the poor and sick was such that his statue was left untouched. This is an eloquent testimony to a man who personified the humanity of the Son of God. It is said that when he served the poor, he 'touched God' and when he came before God, he found himself reaching out to the poor.

St. Vincent died while sitting in his chair on 27 September 1660, in his eightieth year. It is recorded that his last words were, 'I believe, I hope, Jesus.' His feast day is 27 September.

Sr. Catherine Prendergast, D.C.
Dublin, Ireland
8 November 2005

QUOTATIONS OF

ST. VINCENT
DE PAUL

IN THE SERVICE OF GOD

... when you leave prayer and Holy Mass to serve the poor, you are losing nothing, because serving the poor is going to God and you should see God in them.

IN THE SERVICE OF GOD

Do not rest content with doing good,
but do it in the way God wishes;
that is to say,
as perfectly as you can,
making yourselves
worthy Servants of the poor.

IN THE SERVICE OF GOD

Servants of the Poor,
that is the same as saying,
'Servants of Jesus Christ'
since he considers as done to Himself
what is done for the poor,
who are his members.

FAITH IN ACTION

Say little; Do much.

FAITH IN ACTION

Good works are often spoiled
by moving too quickly.

FAITH IN ACTION

As long as Charity, Humility
and Simplicity
exist among you
one can say:
The Company of Charity is still alive.

FAITH IN ACTION

You have no right to anything
but food and clothing;
what is over
belongs to the Service of the Poor.

FAITH IN ACTION

May our presence and care
to those most in need
reflect the gentleness,
esteem,
and dignity we see reflected
in the life and work
of Jesus.

FAITH IN ACTION

May the radiance of your charity
be a beaming light.

FAITH IN ACTION

We should strive to reciprocate
the marks of confidence and kindness
we receive.

GOD IS THE CENTRE

If God is the centre of your life,
no words will be needed.
Your mere presence
will touch their hearts.

SEEING GOD

Some persons look
and never see,
others see
and never look.

ROOTED IN GOD

Nature demands
that trees be deeply rooted
before they can bear fruit
and this is a gradual process.

THE HAND OF GOD

Always,
the hand of God is outstretched
for those who wish to clasp it.

GOD'S LOVE

If God's love is fire,
then zeal is its flame;
if God's love is the sun,
zeal is its ray.
Zeal is the purest element in loving God.

GOD'S GRACE

God makes use of the humblest
instruments
for the extraordinary operation
of His grace.

GOD'S PROVIDENCE

... you should have
an unshakable confidence
in His Providence,
which will never,
never abandon you.

FINDING GOD

A Sister will go and visit the poor
ten times a day,
and ten times a day
she will find God there.

YOU ARE DEAR TO GOD

... you are as dear to Him
as the apple of His eye.

LEAVE TO GOD

Let us leave matters to God.

NOTHING BUT GOD

The perfection of a Daughter of Charity
consists in this:
to cleave to nothing but God.

UNANSWERED PRAYERS

If,
after so much effort and prayer,
the matter is not successful,
it will be a clear sign
that God
does not will it.

GOD'S CLOCK

The works of God
are not accomplished
when we wish them,
but whenever it pleases Him.

FIRST THOUGHT

Your first thought
should be of God.

ADORING GOD

What do you think
is the meaning of adoring God?
It is to render Him the homage
that belongs to Him alone,
and to acknowledge that
He is your Creator
and Sovereign Lord.

ABANDONMENT

Let us abandon ourselves
to the providence of God
and be very careful
not to run ahead of it.
If it pleases God
to give us some consolation
in our calling,
it is this:
that we have tried to follow
his great providence
in everything.

GOD'S REST

Your nightly duty is laden
with heavy responsibility
and it is only through rest,
sensibly taken,
that you will possess
the presence of mind
your duty demands.

BITTERNESS

Bitterness never served any purpose
than to embitter.

CHOSEN BY GOD

Is not your heart touched at the thought:
'God has chosen
a poor country girl
for so holy an employment'?

STRAIGHT AS AN ARROW

We must go to God
straight as an arrow.

FAITHFULNESS

If we are faithful in small things
God will trust us
with those that are greater.

FINDING GOD

Do you wish to find God?
He communicates himself
to the simple.

RULE WITHOUT WEIGHT

A Daughter of Charity's rule of life
should be for her
what wings are to a bird,
motive force without weight.

ACT TOGETHER

Proceed quietly,
pray a great deal
and act together.

CHARACTERISTIC OF GOD

We must strive to soften our hearts
and make them sensitive
to the sufferings and worries of
the neighbour,
and beg of God to grant us
a genuine spirit of mercy
which is the spirit
characteristic of God.

THE BEST INTERPRETATION

Everything should be given
the best interpretation.
As the Bishop of Geneva used to say,
if a thing could be looked at
from a hundred angles,
we should always look at it
from the best.

UNITY

How can you gain souls to Jesus Christ
if you are not united to one another
and to Him.

THE SPIRIT OF GOD

Be careful not to overdo it ...
The spirit of God leads us on gently
to do the good
which we can reasonably accomplish
so that we can do it consistently
and for a longer period of time.
Act thus ...
and you will be acting according
to the spirit of God.

HUMILITY

A fault may serve for our advancement
when it serves to humble us.

MUTUALITY

Mark you,
your Sister
may perhaps
have as much difficulty
in bearing with you
as you have with her.

GOSPEL OF SIMPLICITY

... God has given me
such a high esteem for simplicity
that I call it my Gospel.

CORDIALITY:

... if charity were an apple,
cordiality would be its colour.

THE PARADISE OF COMMUNITIES

Charity is the Paradise of Communities
and the soul of all the virtues;
and it is the humility,
which attracts souls and preserves them.

A SACRED TRUST

To be involved
in the service of Jesus
is a sacred trust
to which we have been invited.

GIVE AND RECEIVE

There is nothing more in keeping
with the gospel
than on the one hand
to gather up light
and strength for the soul
in prayer, spiritual reading, and solitude,
and then go forth and dispense
this spiritual good to [humanity].

THE POWER OF PRAYER

Give me a man of prayer
and he will be capable of everything;
he can say with the apostle:
'I can do all things in Him
who sustains and comforts me'.

THE GREAT SECRET

Surely the great secret of the spiritual life
is to abandon all that we love to Him
by abandoning ourselves
to all that he wishes,
in powerful confidence that
all will be for the best;
and hence it has been said
that all things turn to good
for those who serve God.

ABUNDANT GRACES

Abundant grace comes ...
only to the humble
who realize
that all the good done through them
comes from God.

PEACE OF MIND

Relieve your mind
of all that is troubling you;
God will take care of it.

THE IMITATION OF CHRIST

He invites you to follow Him
and to imitate Him and,
although you may imitate Him
from afar off,
His goodness and love
is so great
that He is willing to be honoured
by your efforts.

HUMBLE YOURSELF AT THE THOUGHT

Humble yourself greatly ...
at the thought,
that Judas had received
greater graces than you,
and that in spite of that,
he was lost.

THE BLESSED VIRGIN

God always kept alive in me
the conviction
that I would be freed
because of my unceasing prayers to Him
and to the Blessed Virgin Mary,
through whose sole intercession
I firmly believe I was delivered.

CHARITY AND JUSTICE

Charity is not charity
if not accompanied by Justice.

CHARITY IS THE NAME YOU BEAR

Charity is the name you bear.
Charity it is the robe
in which you are clothed
with its three parts:
Love of God,
Love among yourselves and
Love of the Poor.

Vincentian Family

The Vincentian Family, which came into existence nearly four centuries ago, is made up of people and institutions united among themselves with one noted fundamental characteristic in common: that of following Christ, Servant and Evangeliser of the Poor; in the manner of Saint Vincent. The charism given to Saint Vincent is shared, in different ways, by some millions of people.

Three branches of this Family were founded by Saint Vincent:
The Congregation of the Mission (Vincentians)
The AIC (International Association of Charity)
The Daughters of Charity, co-founded with
St. Louise de Marillac.

Other branches of the Family, such as the Society of Saint Vincent de Paul, the Vincentian Marian Youth, The Association of the Miraculous Medal and many others, who were not founded by Saint Vincent, but who are inspired by his spirit, have chosen him as patron or have accepted his rules.

For further information visit *www.famvin.org*

The Little Book of
St. Louise
de Marillac

Introduced by
Sr. Catherine Prendergast, D.C.

Compiled by
Don Mullan

a little book company

First published in 2005 by
a little book company
11 Hillsbrook Crescent, Perrystown,
Dublin 12, Ireland.
Email: info@alittlebookcompany.com

In association with the Daughters of
Charity of St. Vincent de Paul

Compilation copyright © 2005, Don Mullan
ISBN 0-9547047-6-2

Designed & typeset by David Houlden,
PageWorks

Printed by Webcom, Canada

To

The Daughters of Charity
of
St. Louise de Marillac
and
St. Vincent de Paul

On the occasion of the
150th anniversary
of their arrival in Ireland
(1855–2005)

Author Acknowledgements

Sincere thanks are owed to Sr. Catherine Prendergast, D.C., Congregational Leader, Daughters of Charity, Ireland, and Sr. Kathleen Moore, D.C.; for their immense support and encouragement in the course of compiling this small volume of the co-founders of The Daughters of Charity: St. Louise de Marillac and St. Vincent de Paul. Both founders, no doubt, are humbled still by the quality of service they have inspired, some four centuries after their own earthly existence. I am also immensely grateful to Dr. Regina McQuillan who, for two years, wrote to me and telephoned me with encouraging words that this small volume might be produced. I am very grateful to the following members of the worldwide Vincentian Family who sent their favourite quotations from both saints for consideration: Sr. Julia Denton, Marsfield, New South Wales, Australia; Ms. Columba Faulkner, Society of St. Vincent de Paul, Dublin; Denise Gardiner, DC, St. David's, Pembrokeshire, Wales;

Sr. Catherine Gaynor, DC, Blackrock, Co. Dublin;
Sr. Margaret Gilbraith, DC, Christopher Grange,
East Prescot Road, Liverpool; Cora and Danusia
Kaska; Sr. Breege Keenan, Phibsborough, Dublin;
Sr. Mary John Lindner, DC, Maryland Heights,
Missouri, USA; Sr. Patricia McLaughlin, Nausori,
Fiji Islands; Fr. Myles Rearden, CM, Maynooth,
Co. Kildare; Sr. Bernadette Ryder, The Marillac,
Brendwood, England; Sr. Maureen Tinkler, DC,
Vincentian Millennium Partnership, Newcastle-
upon-Tyne, England; and Sr. Rita Yore, Blackrock,
Dublin. I must also thank my sister Moya Mullan
and Mr. John Ryan for assistance with parallel
reading; Seamus Cashman for giving me the
original idea of a little book series on the saints;
Susan Ginch and the staff of Webcom for their
professional services; David Houlden, PageWorks,
for design and typesetting support. Finally, the
Daughters of Charity wish to thank Don Mullan
and his family, Margaret, Thérèse, Carl and Emma
for their encouragement in bringing this little book
to fruition.

Introduction
St. Louise de Marillac

In life and in death, St. Louise de Marillac lived in the shadow of the great St. Vincent de Paul. Yet, the noble movement he inspired, across four centuries and five continents, owes much to her inspiring charisma, commitment and undying energy. Louise de Marillac was, in no small measure, Vincent's guardian angel on earth. She was God's greatest providential gift in the religious life of Vincent. She was, in every manner, his soul mate. With her, they co-founded the Daughters of Charity, 'the servants of the poor', in 1633.

The Daughters wore the peasant costume of the day, enabling the sisters to pass unnoticed in the streets of Paris. 'Your convent', Vincent told them, 'is to be the house of the sick; your cloister, the city streets; your chapel, the parish church; your veil, modesty.'

In a Conference to the Daughters of Charity in 1660, the year of Louise de Marillac's death, St. Vincent said of her virtues: 'What a beautiful

picture, O my god, this humility, faith, prudence, sound judgement, and constant concern to conform all her actions to those of Our Lord! O Sisters, it is for you to conform your actions to hers and to imitate her in all things.'

Louise, who never knew her natural mother, was born on 12th August 1591 in Paris and cared for by her father, Louis, a member of the aristocracy. She was educated at Poissy by the Dominicans, amongst whom, was a grand aunt.

In 1613, the Marillac family arranged for Louise, then 22, to marry Antoine le Gras, a 32-year-old secretary to the Royal Family. They had one son, Michel, born in 1613. Antoine le Gras died in 1625, having suffered poor health throughout their marriage. Louise was 34 and Michel 12. Around this time she met with Fr. Vincent de Paul, a priest who was renowned for his work amongst the poorest of the poor. They became lifelong friends, Vincent acting as her spiritual director. Increasingly she became involved in assisting Vincent with and establishing

Confraternities of Charity. On 29 November 1633, Louise established in her own home the first Company of the Daughters of Charity. As the Company grew they worked with the sick poor, with war refugees and established schools in Paris and their first hospital at Angers, a two-week journey from Paris.

Before dying, Louise witnessed the stirrings of the missionary movement of her Company. Today, some 21,000 members of the Daughters of Charity continue her work in 93 countries across the world.

Her body is preserved at the rue du Bac in Paris, the mother house of the Daughters of Charity.

The feast day of St. Louise de Marillac is 15 March.

Sr. Catherine Prendergast, D.C.
Dublin, Ireland
8 November 2005

QUOTATIONS OF

ST. LOUISE
DE MARILLAC

THE PHILOSOPHER'S STONE

It seems to me,
that you have found
the philosopher's stone of devotion
when the firm resolution to do His will
calms your anxieties.

GOD'S WILL

Remember ...
it is for the accomplishment of His will
that you must work ...
as would an ambassador for a King.
All must be done with
gentleness of heart and humility,
as we consider the interests of those
with whom we are working
rather than our own
or even those of the Company.

GOD'S WILL

If we want to please our good God,
we must not look so much
to what we want to do
but to what He wants us to do.

FOR THE LOVE OF GOD

Take care of yourself
for the love of God
and reflect that one way to do this
is to remain cheerful
by conforming yourself completely
to the holy will of God
and not worrying about anything.

TRANSITION

Do not believe
that things will always be
as they now are.

TRANSITION

You are well aware
that changes are always difficult,
and that it takes time to learn new ways
of serving the poor skilfully and well.

A RELIABLE ADVISER

Your great trials and mental turmoil
in all this confusion do not arise
so much from the uncertainty of events,
opposition and conflicting reports,
as from the fact
that you have no one reliable
to comfort you and give you advice.

DISPOSITION

Ask God
to put us in the disposition
to listen and to endure
all that is said
for or against us
so that none of it troubles us.

LAZINESS

If you are discouraged,
I will tell you
what I have already told you several
times,
namely
that you must work.
Laziness
brings sin to the soul
and illness to the body.

DOING GOOD

When I am accomplishing
some good deed,
I shall develop the habit
of calling to mind
the belief that God and His angels
are watching me.

HOLY COMMUNION

Holy Communion ... causes us truly
to participate
in the joy of the Communion of Saints
in Paradise.
This joy was merited for us
by the Incarnation and the death
of the Son of God.
So powerful was this merit,
that the reconciliation of human nature ...
is so great that we can never again
be separated from the love of God.

BREAD OF ANGELS

O Bread of Angels
may Your precious body,
Your holy soul and
Your glorious Divinity,
which I adore in this Holy Sacrament,
take complete possession of me.

THE HOLY SPIRIT

May I not, beginning in this world
flow into the ocean of
Your Divine Being?
Should I be so fortunate
as to receive the Holy Spirit, oh,
how I must desire this
with my whole heart!

THE HOLY SPIRIT

The Holy Spirit,
upon entering souls
will establish the laws of holy charity
by endowing them with the strength
to accomplish tasks
beyond their human powers
so long as they remain
in a state of total detachment.

THE HOLY SPIRIT

I beg the goodness of our Lord
to dispose our souls
for the reception
of the Holy Spirit so that,
burning with the fire of His holy love,
you may be consumed
in the perfection of this love
which will enable you
to love the most holy will of God.

LOVE ONE ANOTHER

You will love one another
realising that since God has chosen
and assembled you
to render Him the same service,
you must be like one body
animated by the same spirit,
and look upon one another
as members of the same body.

LOVE ONE ANOTHER

Let us truly love each other in Him,
but let us love Him in each other
since we are His.

THE PURE LOVE OF GOD

Let us serve with hearts
filled with the pure love of God
which enables us always
to love the roses amidst the thorns.
How short is this life of pain!
How long,
love-filled and desirable
will be our blessed eternity!

TO LOVE GOD

The desire to love God
and the practice of that love
make all things marvellously sweet!
What a great consolation it is
for good souls to have the opportunity
to prove the love they bear Him,
by the service
that you render to the poor.

TO LOVE GOD AND NEIGHBOUR

Reflect often
that it is not enough
to have good intentions
because,
when we received the commandments
to love God with all our heart,
we also received a second commandment
which is to love our neighbour.

GOD AND NEIGHBOUR

I believe that God,
in His divine love,
desires you to love Him
uniquely, entirely and unselfishly
and to have no other concern
or even satisfaction
except those which pertain to Him
and to your neighbour.

GOD'S GRACE

Use profitably the grace which God has
given to renew you in the spirit
of unity and cordiality that the
Daughters of Charity must possess.
I recommend particularly mutual support
something which is absolutely necessary
since it leads us never to see the faults
of another with bitterness
but rather always to excuse them
while humbling ourselves.

GOD'S GRACE

Does the stronger support the weaker
lovingly and cordially
as the need arises?
I beg Our Lord
grant us the grace
never to violate it.

HUMILITY

When someone
does you the honour
of asking your advice,
answer with great humility.
What do we have
except what has been given to us?
What do we know
except what has been taught us?

HUMILITY AND GENTLENESS

In the name of God,
I beg you to strive to cultivate solid virtue,
especially humility and gentleness.
Do to others as you would
have them do to you.
Above all,
be supportive of them
and welcome kindly
those who might find it difficult
to approach you,
if there are any.

THE HUMILITY OF GOD

The humility of God
who calls us to be perfect
as He is perfect
should give me great courage
and lead me to great purity of intention ...
[God] will never fail to assist me
when He asks something of me
which is beyond my capabilities.

TO RECEIVE THE GRACE OF GOD

Pride and all its effects
are great obstacles
to the action and plan
of God in the soul.
Since I recognise this to be true
in my case,
I shall strive to simplify
the workings of my mind
and to keep it humble
not only in order to receive
the grace of God,
but also out of gratitude for His love.

LOVED BY GOD

The least esteemed by men
are perhaps the best loved by God.

THE MUSTARD SEED

Our Lord wanted to make
the Kingdom of Heaven
accessible to us by comparing it to a
mustard seed ....

... I am well aware that this seed contains
great strength within itself,
both in its capacity to multiply
and in the quality it gives to everything
that is seasoned with it.

THE BLESSED VIRGIN

May all creatures pay homage
to your greatness (Mary)
and look upon you as
the sure means for reaching God.
May they love you above all other
pure creatures
and render you the glory you deserve
as the beloved daughter
of the Father,
mother of the Son
and worthy spouse of the Holy Spirit.

MOTHER OF THE SON OF GOD

Everything is comprised in her title of
Mother of the Son of God.
How admirable are her deeds!
With good reason the Church
addresses her as
the Mother of Mercy
because she is also
the Mother of Grace.

OUR LADY

Let us take Our Lady
as the model for our daily lives
and bear in mind
that the best way to honour her
is by imitating her virtues.
We should particularly honour
her purity
since we are the spouses of Jesus Christ.
We should also imitate her humility
which led God to do great things in her.

GOD WANTS ONLY OUR HEARTS

Speak to God
with great simplicity and familiarity.
Do not be concerned whether or not you
receive any consolation;
God wants only our hearts.

GOD'S MOST HOLY WILL

Upon awakening,
may my first thought be of God.
May I make acts of adoration,
thanksgiving and
abandonment of my will
to His most holy will.

TURN TO GOD

Turn to God at the beginning
of each action;
to make an act of humility,
recognising that
we are unworthy to perform it;
then to make an act of love,
undertaking it for love of Him
and offering it to Him
in union with similar actions
which His Son performed
while He was on earth.

If you realised how fortunate you are
to be in a place
where everything contributes
to your sanctification,
you would praise God continually
for having chosen you for this work.

GOD IS MY GOD

My heart is ... overflowing with joy
on account of the understanding ...
our good God has given me of the words,
'God is my God' ....

THOSE IN AUTHORITY

Those to whom God gives
the charge of others
must forget themselves entirely
and in all things.
Remember
that those in authority
must be the pack mules of the company.

THE POOR

If we forget for a moment
that the poor are the members
of Jesus Christ,
we will inevitably serve them
with less gentleness and love.

THE SERVICE OF THE POOR

I beg you to be an example ...
who is given to God
for the service of the poor
and who, therefore,
must be more with the poor
than with the rich ....

THE IMITATION OF CHRIST

God did not relieve us
of the need to earn our bread
simply to give us a life of ease.
He did so in order
that we might work ever harder
in imitation of His Son.

THE IMITATION OF CHRIST

It is not enough to visit the poor
and to provide for their needs:
one's heart must be totally purged of all
self-interest ...
we must continually
have before our eyes our model,
the exemplary life of Jesus Christ.
We are called to imitate this life,
not only as Christians,
but as persons chosen by God
to serve Him in the person of His poor.

DIVINE HUMANITY

Because I know that God sees all things ...
I should always ... go to Communion ...
solely for the love I should bear
the holy and divine humanity
of Jesus Christ ....

SERVE THE POOR WITH JOY

... to serve the poor with joy, courage,
constancy and love ...
to be very careful
of the goods of the poor
and the interests of the house ...
to be faithful to prayer,
even while coming and going,
if time does not permit you
to make your meditation in the Chapel.

THE POOR

Remember
it is the poor that you serve,
that it is their money you are using ....

LIFE IS SHORT

... the thought we must frequently have
[is] that this life is short
and that well-accepted suffering
leads us happily to eternity.

CONFESSION

Although I speak to you
of going to confession,
I do not want to cause you
to be afraid of death.
I do this because
it helps you to remain
in the grace of God,
so that He may always
watch over you.

THE GUIDANCE OF GOD

Recall the great Saint Teresa.
She was satisfied with the essential
and calmly abandoned the rest
to the guidance of God.

TRUST IN GOD

I must have great trust in God
and believe that His grace
will be sufficient
to enable me to fulfil His holy will,
however difficult it may appear to be,
provided the Holy Spirit
is truly calling me.

OUR VOCATION

Our vocation is not to a parish
or a diocese
but to the entire world.
And what are we called to do?
To do what the Son of God did ...
spread fire upon the earth
so that it might be inflamed with his love.

PRUDENCE

Prudence consists in speaking
only about important matters
and not relating a lot of trifles
not worth saying.

CONFIDENCE

Our Lord asks of us
more confidence than prudence.
This very confidence
will cause us to be prudent
as situations require it,
without our even realising it.
Experience has shown this
on numerous occasions.

A SOLID FOUNDATION

The greater the work
the more important it is
to establish it on a solid foundation.
Thus it will not only be more perfect;
it will also be more lasting.

ALL THAT HE ASKS OF ME

So as not to be taken by surprise
by the uncertainty
of the moment of death,
I shall dispose myself to practise
all that He asks of me.

Daughters of Charity

The Daughters of Charity are a worldwide Society of
Apostolic Life, in community, working with individuals,
families and other groups of people, of all nationalities and
beliefs, who are in need, disadvantaged, or marginalised —
offering support, affirmation and practical help. Motivated
by the love of Christ, we live and pray in community,
supporting each other in our common mission of service.
Our Ministries include education, spirituality, health and
palliative care, social and parish, prison ministry, pastoral
ministry and advocacy for change. As needs change, so do
our services. Our mission calls us to be innovative and
inventive, collaborative and inclusive.

Contact information:
International Headquarters: Compagnie de Filles des la
Charite, 140, rue du Bac, 75340 Paris Cedex 07, France
Tel. 00 33 1 49-54-78-78 *www.filles-de-la-charite.org*

Irish Headquarters: St Catherine's Provincial House,
Dunardagh, Temple Hill, Blackrock, Co. Dublin, Ireland.
Tel. 00 353 1 2882896 *www.daughtersofcharity.ie*